Tales of Two Cubs

Book 1
in the
FOX HOLLOW SERIES

Bonnie J. Gibson

Flint Hills Publishing

Tales of Two Cubs, Book 1 in the Fox Hollow Series © Bonnie J. Gibson 2020

Original art by the author

Gibson Made, LLC

Cover Design by Amy Albright

STONY POINT
Graphics

Flint Hills Publishing

Topeka, Kansas

www.flinthillspublishing.com

Printed in the U.S.A.

ISBN: 978-1-7332035-7-9

DEDICATION

For my husband Jeff, and our magnificent children, Brenton and Taylor.

Down in Fox Hollow, Momma Fox had two cubs. One named Meadow, the other named Brush.

Clever little darlings, right from the start. Meadow could do cartwheels. Brush had a passion for painting.

One day Brush asked Momma, "Did God paint the grass green and the sky blue?"

"Why yes," replied Momma. "God paints in the morning when the sun begins to rise.

God paints in the evening when it's time to say good night.

That's how we know when our day is complete, from start to finish in our work and our play."

Meadow chimed in with a sweet squeaky voice, "Did God paint the flowers yellow, orange, pink, red, and purple too?"

"Yes," said Momma. "God paints in many different shapes and colors to make us smile whether we are happy or feeling a little blue.

Why, here in Fox Hollow, we are all different shapes and colors.

Just like the flowers and the trees.

God loves us for our wonder, for our hearts, and because we are free."

"What does 'free' mean, Momma?" Brush asked before he fell asleep.

"Free means you can be yourself, no matter what others say and think.

It also means that your feelings matter. We should always strive to be free. Free to sing, dance, breathe, dream, paint, learn.

We should exercise our minds, our bodies, and even our spirit deep inside. That will keep you brave, kind, smart, healthy. . ."

Meadow interrupted, "What if I want to keep my feelings to myself?"

"You can certainly do that," responded Momma. "You can let them get jumbled up all together, just like the ingredients in my delicious Fox Hollow Stew.

We all have so many different emotions like happy, scared, and even mad. You can give all those feelings control of your spirit. Or, you can choose freedom."

Momma continued, "Just remember — when your tummy gets too full of emotions, it can give you a terrible tummy ache!"

"I don't want to be sick!" squeaked Meadow.

"Well, of course not, my darling. Explore and share different ways to express yourself so your emotions don't build up inside. That will help keep you healthy and strong."

"Can you rub my tummy, Momma," Brush asked, half asleep. "I don't want my feelings to get all jumbled up inside."

"Me too!" squeaked Meadow.

Momma gently rubbed their little tummies and stroked their tiny foreheads until they fell fast asleep.

The very next morning, Momma awoke and cooked breakfast. She said good morning to Momma Bird who was feeding her babies in a nest nearby.

Quickly, her two cubs met her by her side, Meadow with a lengthy hug, and Brush with a beautiful painting and twinkle in his eye.

"Brush, my artist! Did you paint this late last night while I was sleeping?" asked Momma.

"Yes," Brush said. "I wanted to show everyone in Fox Hollow how all the shapes and colors make me feel on the inside."

"What about me?" squeaked Meadow. "I want to show how I feel, too."

Momma gave Meadow a kiss on the cheek and reminded her, "That's what your cartwheels do."

Brush dipped his tail in the paint, said a prayer, and opened his eyes. Then he painted beautiful artwork with all the joy he felt inside.

Meadow did many cartwheels and chased some butterflies.

Both cubs giggled as they played hide-and-seek. Brush did the counting while Meadow found a place to hide.

Meanwhile, Momma built a fire so they could roast marshmallows before saying good night. The cubs talked about how much fun the day had been.

Meadow began to shiver in the much cooler night air. Momma said, "It's time for bed. Aren't we happy we can all snuggle up in our toasty home?"

Brush and Meadow agreed, "Oh yes, Momma!"

The End.

About the Author

This story was inspired by my creative son Brenton and my beautiful daughter Taylor. Taylor was born with Down Syndrome and a critical, congenital heart defect. After surviving Taylor's early childhood challenges, we are navigating the very unique world of Taylor's adulthood. In this new chapter, I have become joyously aware of the healing power of creativity. I love you, my darlings, and I'm grateful for all you continue to teach me.

Momma
Bonnie J. Gibson

Taylor & Brenton Gibson, the author's children.

For more about Bonnie and her work:
www.gibsonmade.us
Instagram@lifeacanvas
Facebook: Bonnie J. Gibson Author (@BonnieJGibson)

COMING SOON!
Book 2 in the Fox Hollow Series
Tales at the Lake

Made in the USA
Middletown, DE
12 July 2020